A

HEARING HEART

BOOKS BY DANNY SIEGEL

Essays	1980 -	ANGELS*
	1982 -	GYM SHOES AND IRISES* (Personalized Tzedakah)
	1987 -	GYM SHOES AND IRISES - BOOK TWO
	1988 -	MUNBAZ II AND OTHER MITZVAH HEROES
	1989 -	FAMILY REUNION: Making Peace in the Jewish Community
	1990 -	MITZVAHS
Poetry	1969 -	SOULSTONED*
	1976 -	AND GOD BRAIDED EVE'S HAIR*
	1978 -	BETWEEN DUST AND DANCE*
	1980 -	NINE ENTERED PARADISE ALIVE*
	1983 -	UNLOCKED DOORS (An Anthology)
	1985 -	THE GARDEN: Where Wolves and Lions Do No Harm to the Sheep and the Deer
	1985 -	THE LORD IS A WHISPER AT MIDNIGHT (Psalms and Prayers)
	1986 -	BEFORE OUR VERY EYES Readings for a Journey Through Israel
	1991 -	THE MEADOW BEYOND THE MEADOW
	1992 -	A HEARING HEART
Midrash and Halachah	1983 -	WHERE HEAVEN AND EARTH TOUCH (Book One)*
	1984 -	WHERE HEAVEN AND EARTH TOUCH (Book Two)*
	1985 -	WHERE HEAVEN AND EARTH TOUCH (Book Three)*
	1985 -	WHERE HEAVEN AND EARTH TOUCH SO9URCE BOOK (Selected Hebrew and Aramaic Sources)
	1988 -	WHERE HEAVEN AND EARTH TOUCH (Combined Volumes: Book One, Two and Three)
	1989 -	WHERE HEAVEN AND EARTH TOUCH (Combined Volumes) in Hardbound Edition
Humor	1982 -	THE UNORTHODOX BOOK OF JEWISH RECORDS AND LISTS (With Allan Gould)

*Out of print

A
HEARING HEART

POEMS BY
DANNY SIEGEL

THE TOWN HOUSE PRESS
Pittsboro, North Carolina

I would like to thank the following people for their help in making this book come to fruition: Allan Gould, Joël Dorkam, Mark Stadler, David Morris, Beth Huppin, Arthur Kurzweil, Louise Cohen, Kate Kinser, Rona Dosick, Steve Vinocor, Jay Masserman, Rabbi Steven Glazer, Rabbi Ron Hoffberg, Amy Ripps, Aron Hirt-Manheimer, and, of course, Dear Old Mom. Each of them read part or all of the manuscript at different stages of its development, offering suggestions and helping me make the final selection for this volume. After the initial inspiration, revising, correcting, and proofreading often cause the poet to lose perspective. Their clear vision of which poems were appropriate for this book can be seen in the following pages. I am grateful.

First Printing 1992
Cover by Fran Schultzberg

Library of Congress Catalogue Card Number: 92-61112
International Standard Book Number: 0-940653-33-8

For Ordering Books:
The Town House Press
552 Fearrington Post,
Pittsboro, NC 27312

For Jay Masserman
Fine Physician and Teacher
Good Friend
Mensch

Table of Contents

King Solomon Asks for a Hearing Heart

(I Kings 3:9)

O God, give me a hearing heart.

Let my heart hear the wings of the hawk,
the crane, the eagle and the owl,
the angelic reds and blues of the macaw,
the angels.

Let my heart hear the tides,
the sap flow to syrup in the trees,
the fires in the rock in the heart of the earth,
the conversations of stars.

Let it hear sweet Torah,
truths unshakable,
prophecy alive.

Let my heart, human, hear tearing hearts
in the final stages of repair,
tears wiped away by kindly hands
soft as irises unfolding.

In whatever my heart hears,
let me hear Your voice.

Prayers and Speeches

Above All, Teach This Newborn Child

Above all, teach this newborn child to touch,
to never stop,
to feel how fur is other than the leaf or cheek,
to know through these hands diamond from glass,
Mezuzah from anything else in the world.
The same with Challah and a book.

As the baby grows,
teach this child to embrace the shoulders of another
before sadness brings them inhumanly low,
to stroke the hair softly of one younger who is weeping,
one older who cries.

Let these hands be a gentle Yes
when Yes is the Truth,
and, gently, a No when No is right.

Whatever these fingers touch —
may they be for new holiness and blessing,
for light, life, and love.

Amen.

Special Bar Mitzvah Speech
By a Young Man With Down Syndrome,
Written With the Help of His Parents

I do not like most labels,
most of all this term: DD.
I am not some developmentally delayed creature today.
Today I am a full-grown Jew.
Do not reach for your Kleenex;
be no more moved to joy for my Bar Mitzvah moment
than for anybody else's with a quicker mind.
There is nothing special about me today.
I came of age.
I recited my blessings.
I joined the congregation.
It is all natural,
though I would not have known this
without my teachers' and my parents' help.

Expect no less of me than of yourselves,
and no more.
My genes specialize in open love and kindness.
For this, do not admire me from a distance.
Do not wish another chromosome for yourself.
All is not beautiful,
even to me,
but it is more beautiful than you allow yourselves to see.
This face, distinct and smiling, feels pain,
but I can manage.
You, with your own, do the same.

Triumph.

My message: Be like me if you can.
Hug.
Smile at the dumbest things.
Give, and do not ask so many questions.
Be good Jews.

I need *you*; *you* need *me*.
If I am out, you are no-one;
in, we are The People God chose when He chose Abraham,
all Jews.

No one is special.
Everyone is special.

Now let us hurry up and finish
so we can get to the Kiddush.
It's been a long morning,
and I am getting hungry.

Bat Mitzvah Speech
Of a Fifty-Year-Old Woman

I wanted this to be in public,
no less than an anniversary I celebrate
in the midst of my family and friends.
I wanted my People to see
I have studied and prepared and rehearsed my readings
no less than my children did for their celebrations,
but, for my part, done with no reluctance.
I did this out of love, because I love my People,
and I see myself more clearly — because of my People,
and I am more myself because of them.

I never had a Bat Mitzvah.
I was born in Wartime.
My parents lived through the Depression,
a time of despair and uncertainty I cannot imagine or feel.
Other things were more important then,
and I do not fault them their choices.
I cannot conceive of joblessness or Europe in flames,
cannot understand what it was like to get up day after day
with the smoke and clouds blocking the sunlight.
I think they are proud of me today,
and I do not want them to feel any guilt
that they never sent me to Hebrew school.
They taught me to love Judaism and Jews,
and I suspect they knew one day
I would make up for lost time.
I am doing that now,
and I am proud to be standing here before you,
my congregation,
feeling somewhat like I felt at college graduation:
this is commencement.
After the Kiddush and the good wishes
and the contributions you have made in my honor
I will continue my study of Torah
as I did yesterday and the day before.
I am just beginning,
and I am only a few years behind Rabbi Akiva
who couldn't read Hebrew until he was forty.

To my teachers:
My gratitude.
My soul is warm.

To my husband:
My thanks,
for your patience and help
and your willingness to be my study partner,
not out of tolerance,
and not from a sense that sooner or later
I would snap out of this,
but, rather, out of love.

And to my children:
Know this —
whichever way you go as Jews in your own lives,
this is not just "Mommy's Jewish thing",
like tennis or wanting to be the best lawyer in town.
It is more than that:
It is Myself, a finer I,
and I wish you the same joy I feel today
all the days of your lives.

Judaism is a jewel, a beautiful diamond.
Jews are the setting for a ring or pendant.
Together, they dazzle the human soul.
I stand here before you dazzled by it all.

May God grant us the greatest gift of all —
peace —
speedily
and in our own time.

Amen.

A Hearing Heart

Statement by a Woman
Who Has Chosen To Be a Jew

I began this journey because I loved one Jew.
I sometimes imagine that, at least at first,
our ancestor Sarah might have done the same,
following her man from Haran to Canaan
through all the hardships and terrors of ancient travel
because she loved him no matter what his ideas or voices,
or perhaps precisely *because of* his ideas and voices.
Now that is no longer good enough for me.
Now I love not only the man I chose to marry
but also the Jewish People, my People.
Where they go, I will go,
and if that means estrangement and exile,
I choose to be the stranger and the exile with them.

I have left my family to be at one with you.
I would not lie at this most awesome moment
saying it is, has been, or will be easy.
Whether they understand or not is not irrelevant,
for they bore me and raised me,
wished only the best for me, and loved me.
They are my parents.
Whether or not they stand by me
as I assume my Judaism —
they will always deserve my love in return.
But *you* must stand by me, *you*, my People,
for you have known the heart of the outcast.

I have been warned:
when the hate of Jews appears in any its many faces,
each one uglier than the next,
and when it roars and growls in its most grotesque voice,
I know:
the curses and stares,
the primitive arrows of old
and the most modern and sophisticated weapons of destruction
are aimed at me.
I cannot hide any more.

Today I cease to be safe,
as I once was in my other life.
Wherever *you* are shut out, *I* am shut out,
and I accept that
as much as I accept all promised joy
that comes to me as a Jew.

If — sitting across the room at some dinner
to raise funds for threatened Jews —
you see this face,
so different from those all around me
because of my Irish grandparents,
I am not a guest or mere sympathizer.
I *belong* there.
Your tragedies of old and of today are mine;
I take them as I take the Simchas:
the Land of Israel, Mitzvahs, Shabbat in all its glory,
foods no longer permitted
now that I have walked ever so proudly over the line.

This week in the Sukkah,
I will revel in God's care,
remembering how fragile our defense is
against the mighty winds and threatening storms
that often frighten us.

I take the name Ruth as mine.
On this most meaningful day, you are my Naomi.
May I and my children be worthy parents
of the Redeemer of Israel.

Amen.

A Hearing Heart

Commencement Address
for Rabbinical School

Understand that all is God's glory,
you, yourselves, an angelic part of it.
Play your part with might, mind, heart, soul and inspiration.
If you will be with God,
God will be with you.

Shepherd your sheep each moment
as if all the world's holiness, all of history's,
depended on you.
It does...
on how you sit with the mother at Shiva
whose son lies miles away in no more than pine slats for a bed,
linen for night clothes,
on how you stand close to the bedside
of those who lie in agony and fear of death,
on which ancient words of hope you whisper to the weary of soul,
on how you touch the disheartened,
on the openness of your house, hand and heart,
on how you make peace.
If you are with your people in good faith,
God, Who redeemed us from Egypt and its agonies,
the taskmasters' tortures and whips,
God will be with you.

Teach all students Torah joyously
and as if your life depended on it.
It does;
and bear that responsibility as privilege.
Few are called to interpret,
fewer to enlighten.
You are of that age-old holy assembly
that counts among its members
giants such as Hillel, Rashi, the Baal Shem Tov,
and others whose names are so many
no human mind can hold them in without the outlet of tears.
They are smoke.

Where holiness hides in shadow, bring the light.
Where it cringes, afraid to show itself,
be strong and comforting.
Set it at ease, holiness.
Embrace it, if you must, in all its loneliness,
until, its weeping through,
it walks with you in your own footsteps
when you walk by the way,
and shimmers in your face
when you lie down and when you rise up.
In your being, be for the sake of Heaven.
In this, too, God will be with you.

Give of your money, the tool of justice and compassion,
and stretch your arms full stretch to those who suffer
as the Almighty God did for us
when all Pharaohs were brought low in our own sight.
The ways of Tzedakah are pleasantness,
and all the paths of Mitzvahs are peace.
Give of yourselves and thereby be yourselves.
Be strong.
Love God.
Love the People Israel,
and be you holy unto them.

God is with you.

Speech to the Camp Counsellors
Just Before the Kids Arrive

I knew some of you in your cribs
when all you could do to entertain yourselves
was stare at a plastic mobile
hanging over your heads in the crib.
I watched some of you play with rattles.
This was before you could say three words.
I used to push some of your strollers to synagogue
as your parents walked beside me teaching me sweet Torah.

Now this camp is yours.
The campers are due to arrive in a few hours,
and if,
in a year,
some wear their Tallis with greater ease,
in five, send you copies of their grades in Hebrew
and flyers from their food drives,
in twenty, send pictures of their children
tasting the lick of honey from their Alef-Bet books,
stand at your bedside in your illness,
stroking your arm gently,
it is you-in-them at work.

You are every teacher's dream class:
in commitment, unsurpassed,
craving — far ahead of me at your age —
a world of Menschen, of Menschlich acts,
of Yiddishkeit flourishing and luxuriant
as the most productive field of grain, once sand,
any farmer in the Negev ever dreamed of.
I wish you had been my counsellors when I was eight.

I conclude with a photograph:
This is my father, screwdriver still in hand,
and this, the moment of illumination:
At the very instant the picture was taken,
he had just removed the training wheels from my bike,
set me on the seat,
and gave me that cosmic, parental push
we all remember.
In the picture (as you can see),
he has followed me the first few feet,
then stepped back.
Frozen in time in black and white,
you can see his hand still six inches from my shoulder.
This is my father.
This is you.

Poet's Prayer

As, for the sake of the poem's meaning,
some must ask who is Xanthippe or Sisyphus
or which gods or goddesses
did which capricious acts
to make their passage of mythology happen,
or ask how hyacinths and zinnias differ
in fragrance, color and line,
so may a generation arise
not knowing pantry from soup kitchen from shelter,
never having seen what we have seen:
women and stunted children staked out
on their heating grates for the night,
eyes a darkening emptiness,
hearts slowed beyond the danger point
from the cold bite of December tearing at their chests.

Speedily may it be.
Soon.
Now. In our own days.

Amen.

Mitzvahs

Mitzvah Therapy

Then let us, troubled, do this:
raise finches and parakeets for all Old Ones living all alone;
tend plants and flowers,
violets and geraniums, impatiens, pansies, and irises,
and roses of every color
to grow to give to the lonely of this world
that they have the will to awaken tomorrow and live;
train dogs to pull wheelchairs
when there is no power in the human's legs
to stand or to walk,
train them to run to their owners
when there is someone knocking at the door
but there is no hearing to hear;
groom horses,
Morgans and Quarter Horses and Welsh Ponies,
that will, in their mass and rhythms, and displaying their style,
trot and canter and gallop
and bring dead limbs back to their rightful lives;
let us clean their stables and pitch their hay
and haul their water to the troughs
so they may be mighty Mitzvah steeds
for, though we drop from exhaustion,
we will have done our part;
tune cars at cost or for free
for all who live so close to the edge of poverty they despair
when all they need
is nothing more than a wreck with four wheels
to take them to work
— for anyone who has only one last chance left;
collect millions of pennies,
count them and roll them and give them away;
be huggers at the Special Olympics,
overcoming our fear of touch;
paint the planes that fly hearts and lungs and kidneys
up and down the coast and cross-country
and everywhere in between,
wherever the desperate are waiting;
clown in the hospitals,
do some things all good.

Thanksgiving Day

The shelters serve early in the day,
noon, most of them.
It is so the volunteers can serve
and talk and listen,
touch and be touched,
and wash and put away the platters and pans,
be themselves human, family and common to all
without rush,
then return to their own homes
and, worthy of the meal's abundance by dint of Mitzvah,
and humble,
give thanks.

Anticipating Answering Today's Mail

I will tell you where to send your wedding dress for poor brides.
Though you will never know their joy,
I can assure you it is beyond imagining,
an arc of the bluest Heavenly blue
in an otherwise brutal sky.

To you, a reference to an adoption service,
but I have no money in the fund
for your dyslexic daughter's private lessons.
I am out.

A check, Mr. C&P Telephone,
for the money I owe for calling my friends,
and to Ms. Visa
for all my vacation fun sunning myself at the beach.

But first, to you:
I am well and doing well,

and last,
may your mother find peace in the Next World
as she never found here on earth,
and may you be comforted among all who mourn
for Zion and Jerusalem.

Letters From the Primitive People

Most, I love Tzaddíkim who cannot spell.
When they write,
they mix "their" and "there"
and "who's" and "whose".
"To" "too" and "two"
and "ible" and "able"
are beyond them.
Apostrophes spill out in all the wrong places
in their letters.

Innocents. They are children,
knowing no more than to make nice to baby,
baby-poor, baby-hungry,
baby-lonely who needs a hug.

The Member of Our Congregation

She had not been much for grades,
and, never one to be a leader,
she had held no synagogue or sisterhood office
all her years as a member.
Comfortably settled on the other side of fifty,
she displayed her daughter's Phi Beta Kappa key
in one of those glassed-in cases guests were required to admire
as a kind of admission fee for one of her dinners.
It was propped up alongside some of the hand-painted figurines
she had collected over the years.
She was proud of it,
though she did not live through this child,
nor, for that matter, through any of her other children.
In turn, they did not look down on her
for being average in the common way of things.
What she was good at, they liked,
though there was never anything so striking in the larger sense:
no big deals or scores of music to her name,
no plans laid — even in remote dreams — for a novel
or to be fabulously rich.
If anything, she was admirable in being so content.

What she did, she did well:
clean house,
even while on the phone and exchanging innocent gossip,
cook the full range of meals
that would satisfy
guests who fancied themselves meat-and-potato he-men
as well as delicacies for the most fastidious gourmand.
And shop a grocery store! — in that, she was no less adept
than a general deploying his troops before battle.

Which is how the free home cleaning-and-cooking service
for people with AIDS all began in our congregation.

And it was in no way out of a sense of boredom or desperation.

One day, the kids being all grown and out of the house,
she just knew she was the best at something
but had been looking in all her Self's wrong places.
In the entire congregation there really was no one
who could straighten a house to the owner's liking
as well and as quickly as she,
leaving more than enough time for light conversation,
no one who could pick up as subtly as she could
on which vegetables were someone's favorites
and which were downed merely to be polite,
and, besides, to know which noshers preferred
to lick the pan with the dough
more than eating the cookies themselves,
and, accordingly, leaving that much more in the raw
and making sure to add extra chocolate chips.

It was in her to recognize these small things
as something of far greater significance,
though they were too often taken for granted.

She is what became known around the synagogue as
The Late Bloomer,
and she went to every funeral and wept for each one of her people
from deep in her heart
— just one more aspect of her genius too long ignored,
and much admired and needed by all of us
who know her and learn her Torah
of the holiness of cleaning bed pans
those extra few special strokes of the rag.

Tzedakah Is All Rage

Tzedakah is all rage:
rage that people must run all over Creation
to gather every little spark from the First Light
God scattered in the worst places;
rage at Life's rules of some poor,
some smashed to inhumanly tiny pieces;
rage against the psychiatrists
who can't seem to tell us once and for all
why some people use their power, great or small,
to kick people around and kick them again when they are down;
rage that there is never enough money at the right moment
to save all wrongfully-dying infants in the world from death,
and that there are never enough
hours in a day
or days in a year
or years in a lifetime
to make some significant dent in the walls of human cruelty.
Cruelty is as hard as diamonds,
but Tzedakah should be the perfect blade
that cuts the ultimate exquisite facet
that makes the gems fit for human and Divine crowns.

Poetry is all peace.
When I am finished with the day's writing,
I am ready for Paradise.
One wonders — poets wonder in particular
(and some with good reason) —
if we aren't like gutter drunks, low and withdrawn,
in an eternally warm and generous fog,
comforting as a blanket on a freezing Winter's night,
warm as Mommy.

Poetry is all peace.

The Night My Hosts Told Me Stories

How they knew I would be in the mood that night
for the coffee flavored with almonds and chocolate
I don't know.
I usually avoid it.
It is usually too sweet for my taste.

How they knew to invite all the right people,
I don't know;
but they did,
and we sat for hours speaking of Mitzvahs,
of jobs for the despairing,
of overcoats and hot coffee on cold nights on the streets,
of toys for the children of the alleyways,
of worn and ragged people taken in to comfort and warmth,
of access for the ones who hear
by the sweep of the hands,
and others who read their prayers in words
printed in colossal letters,
and still others who join in the congregation's celebrations
because of a ramp.
They told me stories more beautiful than any I had ever heard,
and I recall saying to myself afterwards,
"If these stories were flowers,
it would be like seeing all the azaleas in Georgia in full bloom
at one sweep of the eyes,"
and something like,
"If the fullness of life were like a fine cup of wine
overrunning the brim,
these moments would be
the very embodiment of the Twenty-Third Psalm."

And when the woman had finished
The Tale of the Old Lonely Woman Who Was Lonely No More,
we were weeping the finest tears of our lives.

The Rich Entertainer

What she liked most was disarming us.
There was that night I was in a bad mood already
because she had forced us to rent tuxedoes
and our wives had to put on their finest gowns for dinner at her house,
a small dinner at that, no more than ten in all.
We had to sit there all stiff and formal
while her half-breed Dachshund sat there on a chair just like ours
and ate the same food as we did, and on the same plates as ours.
And it kept barking
whenever we tried to make a particularly strong point about our cause...
besides her sitting there herself
in a pair of beat-up jeans and old flower-child T-shirt
left over from her days at the anti-war demonstrations at Michigan,
something she must have picked up for a few dollars
at a second-hand hippie clothing store
or took in a trade for a hash pipe.
Still, her money was good and abundant and honestly come by,
and camp for kids on dialysis or wheelchairs for poor elderly people
or whatever the great needs were at the time
were indeed very great needs.
So the rules of the game had a high seriousness about it
because of the Mitzvah of the moment,
and that day's particular cause had always appealed to her,
and, besides, on the Great Scale of Indignities
it wasn't very much to complain about —
her being so odd and all —
because there was never any cruelty about it,
and we got to being charitable about her back at the office,
calling her merely "eccentric",
which really was the case
since she wasn't being malicious or anything like that,
not even weird or particularly strange.
Just eccentric in a harmless sort of way.
Money does that to you, Tzedakah money in particular,
and, as I said, we needed those wheelchairs
or the new dining hall for camp
or the truckloads of jeans
very badly
at the time.

Light

This is the way it always used to work, until I noticed a change:

As I would drive past the gate and into my parking lot, which was all walled and covered in concrete, my radio would fade out gradually, replaced by static that always irritated me. The signal grew so weak the newscaster's words became unintelligible.

But one day it didn't happen that way.

It was because I was listening to FM instead of my usual AM station, and, even though I was in the same garage, the radio was still clear, still blaring its bluegrass music — some sad theme about Momma's trials after Daddy had gotten drunk one last time, then walked out, and she, the daughter, the singer, just *had to* pick up a guitar (which country singers always pronounce on the first syllable) and write that song. (The singer was singing — as is always the case in these tragedies — with the voice of a young child.)

I found this kind of strange, like when you are travelling somewhere and among the faces you see on a bus you notice one so asymmetrical you wonder how genes get so mixed and mixed up, or — if you are not mechanical — you get to wonder how the torque in a transmission works, or what UFO's really are if there are not really UFO's. That was how I felt that day in the car when I couldn't figure out how the guitar and vocals fly through the air from halfway across the city and then, still with enough vigor in their souls, squeeze through obstructions so solid and thick your head would break open if you fell against them.

Now imagine a room, all dark, within a room, also all dark, within another, three times black. That is the soul undone.

Imagine, again, a candle outside these rooms, its light breaking through, why and how of little concern for the moment.

That light is Mitzvahs.

Or imagine how, on the dark sector of orbit, imagine for a moment that an astronaut has a flashlight in his hand. How far will he see on a space walk? As far as the side of the cargo door? At most, ten feet beyond? But certainly not to the moon.

The light that is Mitzvahs, in the other hand, is measured on a scale that is one dimension or power beyond candlepower or light-years. Whereas starlight turns back on its course, having run its race to the edge (somewhat like a rubber band snapping back on itself), this light travels yet further, to an infinity for which no mathematician modern, medieval, or ancient has invented symbols.

Finally, imagine a room in some palace. In this room are many lights, so many in fact, you would think one more candle's power would be swallowed up and go unnoticed forever. This is not so with the light of Mitzvahs: each new candle doubles the light in the room and changes the hue of the total radiance to an ever-softer and more soothing brightness.

None of this makes any sense to us, just as, when we try to explain FM waves, we are only describing *how* they work and not *why* this is the way the world operates, or should operate, at all. The Hand that molds different radio signals also makes different lights, and if the human eye, even the human mind's eye, cannot picture that kind of brightness (at least for now, in this life), it is enough that the Eye of the Creator can.

Family

Talking to My Grandfather

I was trying to reach my grandfather this morning.
I needed to talk to him.
He would have been 99 on September 12th.

Nothing was working.
I thought I could do it
by remembering the arrangement of his kitchen
and putting him across from me at the table
where he used to read his racing forms
for the harmless two-dollar bets
he liked to place now and again,
ɔut I had no luck.
After I failed with that trick,
all I could come up with, by way of comparison, was:
it was like fiddling with the TV antenna
and still not getting a picture without shadows
no matter which way you turned it or angled the rabbit ears.

Then I tried to remember
the smell of the work boots and gloves in his store,
hoping from there I would see him standing at the cash register
and slipping me a quarter to play the pinball machines down the block,
but that didn't happen either.

I needed to talk to him,
and tell him I missed him,
and how was business?
and did he still have a cold?
and did the optometrist get him his new glasses yet?
and did he want me to come over
to watch the wrestling matches with him
so we could cheer or boo when the champ —
Gorgeous George in those days—
threw the other guy half-way across the ring
or got all bent up in a vicious hammer lock?

I even tried imagining how huge and quiet his old Hudson was,
(picturing the old cars was always a sure stimulus in the past,)
and I would be sitting as straight as I could in the back
so I could reach the windows to see outside
while he got behind the wheel
to take me up the hill to the nice fish place
where, in my mother's absence,
(she had stayed behind for some reason or another,)
he would let me use as much ketchup as I wanted
on the french fries
because that was one of the ways he spoiled me.
But, for the third time, I had no luck,
which, as I write this, seems so wrong,
because I just wanted to talk to him
and see how he was doing.
But, as the writing of poems has its way
of sometimes resembling love,
which, in this case at least,
is also exactly the way life operates —
at the beginning, in the middle,
and sometimes even towards the end of love and of life,
you still might not know how it's going to turn out —
I see just at this moment I had this need to stay in touch
because there were two questions I had to ask,
maybe during the commercials between the wrestling matches:
Is there some form of happiness after you die?
and Was the Talmud right when it said dying
is as simple and painless as pulling a hair out of a cup of milk?

Yizkor 1991,
Looking at My Grandparents' Photographs
Which I Have Brought to Synagogue

So much we owe you:
How we get up in the morning, at six or at nine, or at all,
with the washing of hands and a blessing before food, or without,
even how we hold the fork, right side up, or, European style, over,
when we cut the meat for Shabbas, which we learned at your table.
Because we loved the way you spoiled us,
we watched you closer than a Chássid the Rebbi,
you the parents of my parents.
And *what* we eat: Kosher, watching our watches after meat,
till your time (ours) is right for ice cream.
With you we are always possibly children.

We owe you:
what we sing to ourselves
we remember from the long drives home with Daddy,
what Mommy taught us in the car,
what you learned from your own (mine),
what ours learn from us when we ask,
"Is that that funny language from the pictures, Yiddish?"
We owe you our songs and our speech.
By us, "second nature" is first,
and it is yours.

When we read the news, it is yours,
yours the phrase after turning the pages of *The Times*,
(yours the *Forverts*), asking,
"Is it good for the Jews?" or "When will it ever stop?" meaning:
the trying-and-trying-again to rid themselves of us, the Jews,
all variations of the men on horseback with the clubs and guns
who rode through your town at breakneck speed (your necks),
who drove you here to me, bruised but unbowed.

We owe you our Seders, what we don't skip, will never skip,
where we hide the Matzah, and what we give the children as a reward,
how, opening the door, we look for the horses
and the long knives flashing of the Old and New Oppressors
more, even, than Elijah.

Because of you I do not walk barefoot in the house;
I do not sleep on the ground...because of you.
It is you, you, when I hold the Challah high, and in both hands,
and tear from the center;
you, immigrant Zeyde when my father says, "Poppa",
you, Bobbe, when I hear "Momma",
you, the only ones allowed such holy names;
you, when — all those years I tried to run away —
I still called Friday afternoons to say, "Good Shabbas, peace".
You.
My gratitude, my thanks
when my legs ache more than my stomach
at the end of the fast,
because the last hours of The Day the gates are closing
and it is awesome beyond belief,
and you told me I must stand, and in awe I must stand.
You say, even now, though you are at rest these thirty years,
"Sha! The Shofar. Another few minutes. Sha, Mein Kind, sha."

White as The Marble Throne, as the Radiance itself,
my tablecloth tonight,
bright as your face as you lifted the cup for Kiddush
(which I lift now),
your image, your presence.

We owe, and we repay, with joy.
With these words, I offer you my heart,
which, too, is Yours.

"Hello, My Name Is..."

Their mistake was trifling, really.
It was the Forties and the Fifties
and my parents couldn't have foreseen my Jewish pride rising
like a perfect sun on a perfect Summer's day,
nor would they have had reason to feel the surge ahead of its time
as Israel grew up year by year, no longer a runt to be pushed around,
and balanced on its feet rather like a karate expert,
all firm and ready for all comers
who kept chanting their taunts about pushing the Jews into the sea,
while yet the ultimate host as they brought the people home
from Morocco and Turkey and Yemen
and singles and couples and children
from a Europe that for Jews resembled a torn and bloody Tallis,
the blue and white of its Tzitzit
transferred to the new flag, with a star.

My parents were still recovering from The Tales of the War
and trying to find out about relatives
and learning new terms like "DP"
and absorbing day by agony-filled day
the chaos and devastation of the death camps,
all of which is why, until my Bar Mitzvah,
I was no more than "Danny".

Because of my old name,
I had to fend for myself alone,
just me, myself, a mere "Danny".
Then, in the magical and radical year 5717,
I was called to the Torah, "son of...."
I was linked. I was tied.
I was whatever metaphor put me in line directly with Abraham and Sarah,
and I began to sign my name, even on school reports, in Hebrew,
"ben" comfortably in place in the middle of each phrase.

I picked through all the family documents,
the letters from Europe, the birth and death certificates,
the passenger lists from the boats and papers for citizenship,
until I got the lineage right three generations back
so when people asked who I was, I could say, at least,

Ya'acov Yehudah (of Virginia)
ben Yitzchak Zelig (of New Jersey)
ben Ze'ev David VeTzirel Dvora (of Poland and America)
ben Usher Zelig VeSarah Golda (of the photograph,
of Poland, which was Russia in their day)
HaLevi (of ancient Israel),
and on my Mother's side:
ben Yehudit (also of New Jersey)
bat Shmuel V'Chanah of New York and the neighborhood of Minsk,
even one more, then two more, generations back,
and making a point to rattle them all off at the least invitation
to make myself understood, as in,
"Hello, my name is...
...
...
...
...
...
..., what's yours?"

And I was never alone again.

Gone the Westward Backpacking Hitchhikers

Gone the westward backpacking hitchhikers of yesteryear,
gone the era of free love, lost to disease,
Ginsberg's poems long out of vogue;
my niece takes a course called "Vietnam"
in a suburb not forty minutes from what we call "Little Saigon",
not twenty minutes from where her father and I grew up;
borrows my books, once shocking and fresh, on the war.
I explain why in the world people got married in parks,
the bride in her flower garlands and hand-embroidered dress,
her husband in hand-embroidered shirt.
I explain, "They wrote their own ceremony from Gibran and Dylan.
They may have been barefoot."
In our last few minutes I must make "hippie" mean something,
and I promise to define "Beatnik" at our next get-together,
making a mental note to tell her
that Phil Ochs died by his own hand,
and how, perhaps,
and why, if I can remember...

Just as Mom showed me the old Navy buildings,
still standing after five decades
but still called "temporary" in Washington,
where she did her part for the war effort,
tried to dig up an old ration card in the file drawer,
explained how Dad, the doctor who made more house calls
than anyone in the county could ever remember,
could get more gas than other citizens on the home front,
explained the feel of the day of the stock market crash
and the day the Hindenburg exploded in flame
a short drive from where she lived as a child,
and her then future brother-in-law's midnight runs of bathtub gin,
Roosevelt's pictures sitting down, his death, his widow's face,
Hoover's men gunning down the gangsters
and what exciting news it was when Dillinger met his maker,
what a "hobo" was,
a "Hooverville",
a "gat",
"gams",
demonstrated a Charleston...

Just as her father tried to explain
how the government still conducted its business
even after the President had had a stroke,
and how his brother Otto (whom I remembered) came home
all handsome in a uniform from the Great War
and settled for the rest of his life in Detroit
because he lost all his money in a crap game in that town,
how all those young girls burned in the factory fire
because the doors were locked...

Just as his father before him taught him in Yiddish
the Russian word "pogrom".

Assimilation Sets in More Deeply

Of what will the grandparents speak when they come to visit?
In the next generation, natives of Minneapolis or Dallas,
there will be no European frame of reference.
All home town names will slide off the tongue with ease.
Their Yiddish will be smatterings from *Time* and *Newsweek*,
a word here or there already English, like "shlemiel".
Before Kol Nidre they will say, "Be quiet" instead of "Sha Shtill!"
if they are free that night at all from other obligations,
and since they never knew the difference
between a pushka and a bank on the shelf,
what can be expected two generations down?
Tzedakah will be charity, if that.

The meals they cook as a treat — some specialty perhaps —
will be borrowed from Eastern menus and Italy;
Shabbas lunch will look and taste like Wednesday's,
and they will be good, if slower, tennis partners
than their children and grandchildren.

They will say "Oshwitz" or "Auschwitz",
pronouncing the "w" as "w",
missing the vulgar harshness of the Nazi "v",
the ugly spit in the sound.
Survivors will be defined as anyone
who stuck it out long enough to make it through
a tough accounting course or unfulfilling job or messy divorce,
and there will be no Survivor survivors to correct their terrible error.
Unless otherwise the swelling stream
begins to flow suddenly backwards in its banks,
the little ones at the Seder will never moan,
"Can't we skip the next few pages and get to the food?"
Slender matriarch and styled patriarch won't mind,
and other than candles in December
and gifts given in abundance as if commanded from Sinai
and perhaps an old Purim mask from childhood in the attic,
not much will be left of us.

Relationship to God

Where Heaven and Earth Touch
So Closely, They Appear to be Kissing

In birth, in love,
and in death;
at the horizon (of course),
in the sun's warming the earth so we may live,
in the green leaves' edges
rusting and turning to gold in the Fall,
in bread and its grains and the rains that raise the seed;
in the sapphire and ruby, the emerald and the diamond uncut;
in fingers barely intertwined;
in the red of blood,
the yellow-on-black of the pansies,
the blue of night waters under the rising and risen moon,
the flesh of flesh;
in Torah, in Mitzvahs,
in candles and forgiveness,
in Your never-ending care.

Motzi

You do not bring forth bread from the earth,
unless You mean we, on Your behalf,
sow the seeds, the wheat, the barley, the oat and the rye,
water and watch over the fields,
reap and winnow the grain and sift the flour and bake the dough
because You have endowed us with the wisdom to do so,
and then it is bread You have brought forth from the earth.

You will not bring the Messiah, either, will You?
Unless you mean that we, on Your behalf,
share this bread with the hungry
because You have endowed us with the compassion to do so,
and then You will bring the Messiah
whom we have already brought,
and then we shall all sit at Your table
and eat the amazing loaves of peace.

Little Rituals

...then I pray to God for wisdom;
then I pour myself another cup of coffee.
I may change to my lucky shoes
or open the window wider
to let the chill work through my bones and wake me up,
and sometimes it helps to rearrange
the trinkets on my desk;
then, as sunrise has happened an hour ago
behind my back,
I turn out the lamp
and surrender myself
to God's good light and graciousness;
then I — as another author put it so well before me —
sweat until my life's blood flows from the pen.

The Religious Element of Poetry

However feebly we try,
still, we try to do what any Jew does
flying on the wings of a Tallis:
to hear God.

And that,
as clearly as on those Winter days, chilly and crisp,
when all sound travels from a distance
greater than considered possible for the human ear to hear.

When we write,
we want no less than
good, sweet words from God's mouth to our ears, like,
"Let there be..."
"Let there be light, pure and radiant,
light in and of itself, light and shade, light a reflection of Me."
"Let there be elms and ebony, acacias, elder and butternuts,
all manner of flowers and shrubs, sisal and lilac,
sage, oleander and zinnia, watered by My cooling streams."
"Let there be a multitude of giraffes on the earth's plains,
heads high and majestic on the horizon,
and cheetahs as numerous as the stars in the heavens,
and tigers uncountable as the sands on the seashore,
and great winged eagles above to soar ever closer to Me,
and bringing ineffable pleasure to the human eye."
and "Let there be the eye itself, of man and woman,
to take the delight I give and offer thanks."
and "Thou shalt..."
and "Thou shalt love others...
and "Thou shalt love thy God,
Free Giver of Life."

On Being Asked By One of My Students, "How Do You Say 'Light-Years' in Hebrew?"

You don't,
though it was a good question,
and I am glad you asked.
You don't.
We measure in numbered Heavens, seven in all.
In one of them are the sun and moon and stars.
Something particularly distant
may be said to be in the Third or Fourth Heaven.
Beyond that are angels of varying degrees of importance
with names that usually end in "El",
Gavriél, Michaél, Refaél and the like,
by the hundreds,
and Seraphim all flame.
Farther out still,
on the rim of what we humans call "the universe",
a chariot on a sapphire-colored pavement,
a throne surrounded by tables set for the Righteous,
who are defined liberally in Heaven
as all those who, whatever their gifts,
strove beyond excellence to be kind and just, fair and innocent,
and, on the throne, the Ruler of All the Earth
and All the Heavenly Hosts, too,
yet near unto the lonely and broken-hearted
as the arm of this chair or that glass of tea on the table.
How far that is exactly,
I would be hard pressed to say,
but — to answer your question —
a million light-years, a billion, maybe two,
though it hardly seems to matter.

What You Find

This is what you find
if you live long enough
and if you know where to look
and it is not far,
and the search is not wearing
when you know where to look:
the best.
By which I mean:
people.
By which I mean:
in the people,
some more, some less,
a spark.
By which I mean:
tinder and kindling and glowing coals from Above
throw them off,
invisibly small,
and, once in the soul,
they burn,
and the faces glow.
You do not have to travel as far as I have
to see the faces,
warm your soul by the fire.

Whether It Is Good Enough For Us Or Not

Whether it is good enough for us or not,
they will tell you that
in the multitude of all possible names,
God is nameless.
Whether or not it is unfair to say so,
they will tell you that
the best you can know God
is the way you hear a saw down the block
in someone's garage,
and knowing it is a saw at work,
but having no sense of what is being cut
or to what proportions or purpose,
whether pine for a cabinet,
oak for a dining room table
for years of state banquets in a little castle,
panelling for a den;
or that it is like listening to muffled voices from a distance,
all distorted and muddled,
but the voices are too far away to catch the content of the words
or, for that matter, even which language is being spoken.
They offer you air, fire, light as analogies,
nothing you can hold in your hands,
ether-like, no-things and shapeless.

Our prophets wore themselves out for that amorphous victory.

The best our thinkers can do is,
"As God is kind and caring, so you be kind and caring..."
a kind of endless beginning, a boundless something, high,
and whether or not that is good enough for us or not,
it is where we must begin.

The Chances

When we were children, we had no sense of odds.
In Monopoly, we never thought it would happen to us,
"Go Directly to Jail",
and even when it did,
by the next day we had forgotten all about it,
even if, strange as it was when it happened,
our piece fell on the wrong square two or three times in a row.
And we could play cards days on end,
and one of us lose almost every time,
but, as we saw it,
there was nothing about the cards that seemed of themselves unfair.
The next afternoon we could take up where we had left off
as if nothing unusual or wrong or bad had happened.

You lie in bed, a human image of your diagnoses.
The machine and charts
and the operators of machines and the interpreters of charts
have pronounced their solemn odds — not good —
in the ninety-something to single digit range,
and you put on your best face for me and the rest of your friends
who have come by to say more than hello.
We shift from one leg to another,
stumbling over each other to recite
as if from some Biblical text,
"What a great season the Redskins are having!"
and all chime in about how they stomped Atlanta yesterday,
and, not wanting to hurt us, you ask gently,
"What are the chances the Rabbi was right
back when we were in Hebrew School,
you know, about there being a Next World after This One,
all peace and light?"

Why Synagogues Have Windows

To see the Heavens, of course,
and remember their origins,
and Whose they are, and Whose we are;
to see light and recite Shema, Yisrael-Hear, O Jews!
God is One, is ours, and we belong;
and, at the ending of the light, to begin the day again,
the darkness bringing on another light
— it is always but a few hours away;
to count the stars to close Shabbat;
to love the Creator through blossoms and birds
and through the lowly hedge and the towering trees,
and through the quickening chatter of the woods;
to stand in awe at the snow's silent fall,
and know the Maccabees won because Right makes Right,
says the God of Righteousness;
and to keep one eye out for the hordes, on foot, on horseback,
and to remember, always, the boiling minds
of ancient Pharaohs and latter-day Pharaohs
laying their plans;
to know Pesach is near, freedom is upon us;
to see the commonplace:
business and strolls and shops, the cars, the trucks,
the people in slickers and boots going about their daily affairs
on a drizzly day,
eating and drinking and yet angels in so many ways;
to take what is inside out to the marketplace,
out to the café and the store, and home;
passing by,
to see in,
to go in to hear the words spoken and sung
and to speak and to sing true words;
to remember the source of the light, and the stars, and the blossoms,
and to know the Maccabees' might
is in the light of the Eternal Light,
is in the scrolls in the Ark.

Choices

(After all my years of Torah study, I have still never managed to understand Judaism's "continuum of disposability", other than this: while some things may reach a stage of being no good any more, people are never to be treated as garbage.)

When I die, many are the choices.

We heap the Sukkah's roof in the garbage.
It served its purpose:
adjunct-to-holiness, and, its time up, it is trash.
When I die, will I be like that?

Most people do the same with their Lulav,
though I was recently in a fine house
with de Koonings on the walls and Persian carpets in every room
— the real things —
where Lulavim of years past rest brown in a priceless Chinese vase,
and a very old one at that.
Does God's house look like that?
Do the Tzaddíkim, on their grand tour,
inquire about this anomalous touch to the décor?
The question is then:
how does one achieve this award-of-palm?
Will I be as an old Lulav?

The Essrog.
The Essrog — throw it away,
make it into jelly, a glaze for Shabbas dinner
(a Jewish version of Puritan cranberry sauce),
prick it with cloves and put it in the closet
so the clothes will smell fresh for the holidays.
When I die —
am I to become some thing tossed, some compost,
or will I be a sweetener,
or some kind of refreshing memory to the people who knew me
and will, some day, themselves,
and on the basis of their own stories,
become one of those?

The Tallis, about which there is some ambivalence.
The Holy Society snips one set of fringes
when it lays you out for burial.
No longer kosher, it is yet a fit garment.
Imagine!
All those people walking around the Palace in lopsided Tallaysim!
Is this my metaphor?

Last: a Torah, a Siddur.
We make solemn ceremonies.
They are never — even disfigured or in disuse — trash,
because the Holy Words were in their ink, are still in the ink;
even erased, the Words still have shadows.
That would be my choice, when I die,
if I have to anyway,
pretentious though it may be to compare these kinds of things
that may well be apples and oranges.

Preparing the Body

The Holy Men bathed the face,
then the arms and legs, the chest,
all the while reciting the verses from Psalms.
Moshe lay at rest, over with his sadness.

As the Century, so goes the Tzáddik,
and this one, never one to ask the Great Questions,
went about his way touching and binding and healing as instructed
and according to his strength and sometimes beyond.
Since Nineteen Thirty-Nine, neither he nor the Century was whole,
and his soul had bruises only a shroud could cover.

Friend of the lonely, the immigrant and the sick,
the deaf and the blind and the disheartened,
he is wound now in his pure and simple cloth,
now tied in his white linen belt,
now sent on his way in the most unpretentious of slippers,
sad no more and at peace.

The Life and Death Of a Gentle Man

No one had ever seen him use a knife.
In his house there was nothing sharp,
and even when he would go fishing with friends,
his line had no hook.
He preferred to sit on deck,
gripping the rod lazily in one hand
and gazing as if in a trance at the horizon,
content to hold infinity in his eyes' seeing
just beyond where sky and water met in the far distance.
He died embracing the Angel without hesitation or doubt,
his life full and over,
delighted he had ever lived.

Geography-Geology F1101x

The world is physical and dumb,
though it roar in its tornadoes and floods,
though it drown screams in torrents of water
and crush houses like tinder.

There are names I learned in classrooms
like "yazoos" and "meanders",
rivers and streams rushing and rushing
to straighten themselves out.
They go for the jugular of the banks,
moving rock and soil by law,
always and naturally starting from the weakest point.
So, too, the wind, when it snaps branches
and wears down the most reluctant boulders.
So, too, the cowardly earth's plates when they rise, crack,
make mountains, make mountains disappear in seconds,
and the volcano, without a mind,
choosing the most defenseless fissures
for its surges of fire, its choking smoke.
So Mother Nature.

But there is no sin in weakness.

The Voice commands,
"Seek out the weak, the lowly and breaking,
though not for punishment or curse.
Be unnatural:
bind up the wounds where the flesh bleeds;
repair the tearing seams of the human heart,
lest the flow be fatal;
take the shattered soul,
and, piece-by-piece, apply the touch to make it whole again."

After geology, there is us.

Of Ecological Concern

Along with the endangered owls
and the snow leopards at risk of extinction
and the dying colors of so many species of butterfly,
add this:
the gold-winged human soul.

Miscellaneous

Say There Is Something Priceless
That Has Been Misplaced

Say there is something priceless that has been misplaced
in a huge museum — the size of the Smithsonian, for instance —
something like the Hope Diamond or the Star of India, for instance,
and say there are special dogs trained to sniff out diamonds.
A poet would be one of those dogs,
and the glittering facets of The Beautiful and maybe The True
would be the missing jewels,
and The Holy.

Say there is this mammoth fire in a factory or slum
and three or four people have been burned
down to their teeth as a means of identification,
and say they call in a fire inspector to find the first spark
that caused this dastardly act.
The poet, then, is that inspector,
and the spark is Meaning;
the poet has to describe which side of God's Benevolence this is,
or, of the Divine Attributes,
from which one on the list this tragedy emanates.

Say there is some threat of war,
and the border guards sit at their posts
straining their eyes through those marvelous field glasses
that can read the enemy's communiqués and strategic maps
at six kilometers on a night when there is no moon at all.
The poet is one of those soldiers,
the messages and charts are a "making-sense-out-of-chaos",
a commentary to Torah that must be deciphered.

The poet must know CPR,
must get there no later than one moment before it is too late.

In the Midst of a Kidnapping on the News

To yet have written of flowers and Spring
in the time of torture, the toying with the lives of the kidnapped,
body snatchers, kings and queens every one of them
in their absolute power ever refining their methods,
to yet have written of flowers and Spring is victory,
the pen's might over the sword.
Today's news is the noose that chokes,
the rope that burns the captives' wrists,
the well-turned tongs for pulling nails.
To have written, indeed,
of such as the onset of roses and the revivifying sun
is, at once, a triumph and a comfort,
though it seems evil in its monster shapes wins, will out today.
One might say, on days as these days of terror are,
flowers wilt, even on the page,
and the sun hides in the night.

And still, and yet, to have no hope now is sin;
to wish the dawn,
to urge the flower on and up through the frozen earth
to air and light,
Mitzvah most solemn.

A Recitation for Students of Anatomy

Forgive us.
Forgive us
for what we are about to do.

We pray that you not suffer because of us.
May the work of our hands cause you no indignity.
We mean no harm.

At this most solemn moment,
we swear we shall not forget you.
Your name will be with us
all our days as healers.

Noble and human even in death,
Teacher,
God rest your soul.

Ours and Theirs

Last Fall,
it was clear to me Dear Old Mom needed to get away.
So I took her to Mexico for a week.
One night,
in the lobby of our splendid hotel in Cancún,
three of those fabulous strolling musicians
entertained the guests with their songs,
some of whose words I managed to catch,
songs about love lost, love found, love lost and regained,
and hard work in the fields to eke out a living.
There were the traditional yelps and ai-yai-yais, too.
A couple of days later we went with our driver
to the great Mayan ruins at Chichen Itza.
We were appropriately awed
by the magnificence of it all.
But it wasn't ours.

Last Winter,
I could see my friend Allan needed to get away.
So I took him to Hawaii for a week.
One night,
as the sun was setting millions of miles beyond the beach,
a troupe of hula dancers performed on the hotel lawn.
The torches all around added their special aura,
the dancers (as you would have suspected) were lovely,
their hands and bare feet and hips telling many fine tales
of war and love and sleeping volcanoes and angry volcanoes,
as did the chants and drumbeats in the background.
Earlier, when we walked around the grounds,
we had noticed steam coming up from under some giant leaves
spread over an oven-pit.
We knew they were cooking a pig for a luau.
It was all very interesting;
the dancers, in fact, were exquisite.
But it wasn't ours.
None of it.

One Shabbat,
when we marched around with the Torahs
I overheard some people speaking Russian.
The congregants standing next to them tried to show them
how to take the Tallis and touch the scrolls
then kiss the fringes.
They were hesitant about it,
and their Russian got faster as we walked by their row,
but just as we were about to turn down the aisle,
a daughter, maybe seven or eight, ran out and stood in our way
until we brought the Torahs down to her height,
and she gave them both a big hug.
And she was ours.

The Muse

The moment I saw you gather the centerpieces
to take to the hospital,
you became my muse.
Your friend's wedding was over,
and the band members were putting their instruments away.
No one else was left in the synagogue.

I suspect tomorrow you will be sorting clothes
from a drive you organized for the street children,
or calling friends to raise money for a scholarship for camp,
or, perhaps, laying the table for a dinner for New Americans
who need you.

You inspire.
You are alert to cries and outcries
and attuned to the soul's finest moments.
You tend your Mitzvahs
like a home gardener who succeeds —
even with the worst soils and in a drought —
in bringing forth lilacs and orchids that delight the eye,
yet you leave your guests to discover them on their own.
You are too modest to attribute any of this beauty to yourself.
In your mind, the credit is always due elsewhere.

It makes no difference
if you will ever sit across from me at the table reading the paper
or ask me if my day at work went well
or tell me I look handsome.
Whether or not we ever meet again,
you are mine, forever.

The 12-Year-Old Boy in the Shelter
Talks to the Reporter

*Based on the segment "Shelter Boy" from
the TV news program "The Reporters".*

Why should I make friends?
How can I do it here?
The limit is 30 days,
then we have to go.
We have to go looking for other shelters.

The other kids are always in and out:
their month overlaps with mine only a few days,
and then they move on.
Either one of their parents finds a job
and an apartment somewhere in another part of town,
or they go to a shelter that's different than my next one.
Sometimes they disappear to another city.
Some relative takes them in for a while,
until they get back on their feet.

I remember my friends from before.
We used to play dodge ball for hours after school,
until Mom called me in for dinner.
Now there's no yard to play in,
and it's someone else's food,
though I am old enough to know
the meals are coming from people
who are being kind to us.
Once or twice a kid my age came to serve supper,
and we got to talking afterwards, but I stopped.
I knew after a while he wouldn't be back,
as much as he might have wanted to.
He has school and other things.
He was nice.

Dad never used to make me eat my vegetables.
He used to spoil me.
Now he makes me eat them.
He says I need the extra energy.
Things are different, he says.
I think he needs the food more than I do,
for all those buses and the walking he has to do
to look for another job.
He looks so sad.

Everything's different now.
The kids at school call me "shelter boy",
and it hurts real bad.
They say my father uses drugs.
He never uses drugs.
He never did.
Why do they say these things?
Why do they pick on me so much?

All I have are these, my real friends.
This is Tommy, my tiger, and Ben, my bear.
At least I have them.
I keep them in my knapsack when I go to school.
I never take them out, but I know they are there.
If I took them out,
the kids would take them away from me and make fun.
Then what would I do?
What would I do without my friends, Tommy and Ben?

His Daddy Owned A Buick Dealership

When we were in junior high,
we had a thing about our parents' jobs:
we were especially jealous of one kid, Johnny or Joey or Mike,
because his father owned the dealership downtown
and every year the biggest, newest Buick you ever saw
slid into the parking lot at school to pick him up.
This was when Roadmasters
were only one step down in size from a truck,
snazzier than anything nowadays,
with lots of chrome everywhere, and gadgets.
They drove like a tank,
and you could put the whole team inside, equipment and all.

Others didn't bother us so much:
one was a dentist's daughter.
She would chew her food (as they say in Yiddish) with her own teeth
until she, even a crone, would die,
Bible in her lap in the rocking chair, rocking her way to Jordan's shore.
(She was from an evangelical dental, thumping and shouting lineage.)

And we didn't have any special feelings
for the children of generals and admirals from the Pentagon,
nothing we could hold in our hands,
like the comic books from the drug store owner's daughter
She had a monthly haul of *Superman* and *Captain Marvel.*,
and, as I recall, was quite popular with the boys.
For all the bomb tests of fifth grade —
and we in the Arlington County School System
were never anywhere but Ground Zero —
the officers' gift of peace couldn't be touched
like the flashy grille on the big Buick.
We were, after all, kids,
and, above all, living under Eisenhower in the Time of Good Times.
The bomb tests under the desk were a joke.
Really: what difference did it make if we talked to each other or not
in our squat positions?
If the Russians were going to vaporize us,
what worse punishment could the teacher possibly threaten?

We chose our friends back then by the goodies they could show us.

As singles, we would grow up to do the same.
The criteria were not much different,
at least not on the first round roaming for mates:
professionals, the rich, mavens of stocks and bonds,
mistaking securities for security.
It became part of a warm-up ritual that led to a cynical law:
Never buy an expensive present for a first marriage.

But on the second round, settling down,
and with the body clock picking up its pace,
we looked for others who did not in any way resemble
the exquisitely groomed people we saw in magazines,
who, instead, served huge plates of meatloaf and vegetables
at soup kitchens,
who pulled through divorce settlements with their dignity intact,
who gardened,
who saved strays from the death row of shelters,
who had pushkas on the window sill,
who knew how to dance with a Torah,
who were unafraid to change bed pans
and wash shells of bodies in the back wards of institutions
with a gentle stroke and soothing words.
We looked for the ones who sometimes learned Hebrew late in life,
displaying a quality of courage unlike any other,
who could sit, illiterate but noble,
with pint-sized classmates reciting, "Shin-Bet-Tav — Shabbat!"
(with an exclamation mark),
and, "Shin-Lamed-Vav-Mem — Shalom! Shabbat Shalom!"
And there — in the joy of their voices and with peace on their faces —
the search ended.

A Hearing Heart   *65*

My Students Have Gone Away

My students have gone away.
No, I sent them.
The two of them, my best, are married.
Their families resemble the image of their good hearts.
They want nothing in life but to do good.

They exceed me at every turn,
and my heart rejoices in their kindness and wisdom.

We are left to the telephone and the whim of when to call,
taking care not to disturb family routines.
It would be a breach of an unspoken covenant to say,
"Call me more often, please."
or "Come see me. I need you."

When we meet, we never open a book to celebrate,
though the books we studied are always a part of us,
and if their lives are a picture,
I am off to a corner and in the distance now,
a background to their house, spouses, and children,
if a cartoon, I am far off-center
and with no words in the bubble over my head,
and if a tree, they have come from my seed
but, windblown, flew too far away
for me to watch them
draw earth, air, and water through their roots
to grow mighty and magnificent
and give cool shade freely to others.
Even from my height,
I cannot see them, so far away they flew,
my seeds.

Gems

It comes down to this,
though it is hoped it may never have to go so far:
Family over time has its own concerns and moves away
in the natural flow of years.
It is a legacy of wars and the Sixties,
the accessibility of flights and telephones,
the demands for jobs.
Caprice in the marketplace brings transfers,
has become a law of life of its own, I would suppose.
Get well cards are faxed with ease.
Not to count on family is the safe approach.
Children's lives are their own to live, sadly,
though if they stand with you,
so much the more striking it is,
considering the pull away and away and away.

So, too, with friends:
Seize the pleasures;
hope for the rest.

Fans:
Tastes change,
and the latest poetry in vogue draws them away
to others more of the moment,
though they still speak of the poet with reverence
and the poems with great respect.

Were this the all of it,
one might well look to the future
with no hope at all,
which leaves the students, and theirs, in turn:
They will never abandon the one
who shared such Torah wonders with them.
They have become the gems of words alive,
splendid adornments of old age.

Abraham's Plea

We are soon gone too far.
It will no longer be a matter of ten good people.
It will become a gray time to our eyes,
our mouths and noses masked
against the toxic particles in the air;
it will be a dry time opening the spigot
and praying to the handle for clear, pure water;
the landscape, treeless, will be mere bare scars.
There will be no more metaphors left, lost
"Our love was like a flowing stream,
the salmon gleaming in the sun", gone
"The roses in the garden bloom,
so you, your life so promising."
Like pushing with our whole body against a jammed door,
only to have it fly open opening on a cliff,
we push this earth.

Ten will not do it, fifty;
not long from now millions with all their good will
and their brushes and purifiers and filters will fail
because it has become all just too dirty,
like when we realize it is only three days until Passover
and there is just no time or way to sweep out every corner
and make the house Kosher for the holiday.
It will be the first of many unfit Seders.

The pleas will be heard, but nothing can be done.

Fortieth Birthday Poem
Written Seven Years Late

I would have preferred a few less afternoon clouds
and perhaps being in two places at once:
with my parents in America and at the same time in Jerusalem.
(This was before the little veins in the back of my legs,
and while my best book was at the printer.)
I must have been at my annual festive lunch
at some high-priced restaurant overlooking the Judean Hills.
We were talking about the solid progress we were making
with our careers
and how most wounds in our psyches were healing nicely.
We were doing all right, we said,
and I suppose I was too busy running around
with other friends the rest of the day
to write about it then,
but, the sense of it was, we were,
at least most of us,
doing all right.

Since then, not much has happened:
some more books;
some closeness here and there gained, some lost,
but, on balance, a fair ratio;
some growing fame, at times like a flower,
at times a tree whose roots threaten the basement floor
and foundations of the house;
encounters with more great human beings,
all cordial meetings except one or two;
a changeover of cars with low mileage
just because I could afford it
and wanted to prove something to myself;
a multitude of zeroes and moderate plusses and minuses
on the happiness meter,
and a not-yet-drastic fear of time running out.
In short, a kind of moving with dignity through things day by day,
over 2,000 of them in all,
referring to which, one Rabbi had a kind of motto,
"Blessed is God day by day."

The Visit

Easy at first, the language of friendship
Is, as we soon discover,
very difficult to speak well...
....
and, unless often spoken, soon goes rusty.
(W.H. Auden)

I didn't come because I was in trouble
or had something to say I thought particularly profound.
My work is good and goes well
and I am happy with it.
Nothing spectacular is happening in my life
at this particular stage of things,
but disasters are also, thankfully, absent
and have been for a year now,
and certainly I have not heard of anything terrible —
not since Ron's wife became deathly ill
and he became so sad.
There was nothing we could do for her or for him,
but, as I said, nothing of that order has come up lately.
Nothing at all special is happening in fact,
one way or the other.
I just wanted to come
and know someone within six feet of me cared,
even if we never said anything to each other
and all I did was watch you
make us a couple of sandwiches for lunch
or tinker with the old Jaguar in the garage.

Shabbat and Holidays

In the Presence of Guests,
My Mother Performs Her Weekly Ritual

"There, it's done," my mother said,
spilling a few drops of red, red wine
on the Shabbas tablecloth
in a tone of recitation,
as if it were some holy text.
"Now you may enjoy the meal,"
she said,
imprinting her lesson
of stains, of ownership,
of the soul's relation to God.

The Last Moments of One Particular Shabbas

I. Havdalah in General

Shabbas is the time we take off our masks
and recognize ourselves.
Over, the light is our last gift.

The candle is other, of itself.

II. One Particular Havdalah

We were young and away at some convention,
Our host was not only blind, but blind from birth.
He was famous for something, a man of stature.
This was his first Havdalah, and he seemed at ease.

When he felt the heat on his fingers,
did this satisfy the blessing?
Are light and warmth that close?

We were so young and so new to this.
Were we wrong to stare at his face?

Should the Prayers Fall Flat
On Rosh HaShana

Should the prayers fall flat,
and should the congregants not sing
when I want them to and need them to
because the Hebrew is foreign
and two full generations a language not their own,
and should the sermons fall flat,
as it often does,
there is still the baby crying in the stroller in the back.

Once — in the years of fear —
I visited the synagogue in Leningrad:
all old men
and a row of women in their seventies and beyond,
upstairs in the balcony.

When the words fall flat,
as they often do,
there is still that one good cry
so far from where I stand in the front
I am unable to orchestrate the service
and I feel like a washed-up conductor
with an orchestra that has forgotten the feel of its instruments...
so far from me I cannot see
who it is or whose
or why it is making such beautiful noise,
that one passionate cry of hope.

High Holiday Prayer

O God, do not give me the prize — a year of life —
because a Righteous One declined
out of pity for me.

Let me not be pathetic in your sight,
but, rather, some ways worthy.

In Your humanity, bend,
but only slightly,
for my sake.

Kentucky

These are the hollows of the hack,
where dust from the carbon dark of centuries is not innocent,
not the bothersome accumulations we Spring-clean away for Pesach,
wiping the sills, shelves, and nooks with a smooth cloth
and it is done with.
No cloth cleans these lungs.

Though *I* have not been down in the mines,
we have, we Jews.
It is the same old story we know so well from the Seder:
hauling the pyramid blocks, placing them by whips' measurement,
we slaves, a hundred shoving at a time for each, and weighing less,
are in fair range for chinks and bits flying by their own rules.
Our youth is gone in double time
as our wives watch us slow to a step or two, then collapse.
Our children, lifting us, become determined.

Why T.S. Eliot Was Wrong

April is not the cruellest month.
Passover is not cruel.
The promises of freedom,
though deferred a year and another, a century,
hold good.
God is to be trusted.

All is surmountable; we say all of it:
slave mentality pulling us back to servitude;
the desire, unnatural once free, to be nondescript,
like when azaleas, after the flowers have fallen,
the bush becomes not much more than any other bush;
the price in lives...
all worth some value we cannot measure by any instrument,
by the mind even at its best.

Hope wins.
Hope wins, not because all alternatives are too crushing to consider.
Hope wins in April because it is supposed to win;
it is the stuff of being human,
and as long as there is a Seder
and a child to ask
and a parent to tell the tale,
then, to paraphrase a more correct
though, perhaps, not as dazzling a poet,
hope will spring eternal in the human breast.

Europe

Mother as Young Woman

First I loved your face.
Those angles and the white.
Even then, I suspected you had some Dutch blood in you;
this, even before we had talked
and you described your mother's conversion
as she had told it to you when you were old enough
to ask why her English was so different
from the way your friends' mothers spoke.
At that time
she also explained to you about the War
and how dashing your father had looked in his GI uniform.

We went a little further than that in the next few weeks,
but since neither of us was willing to invest in each other
that little bit of holiness remaining in our souls,
we stopped, by mutual agreement, our moves toward love,
and now all I have left is your face,
that is to say, your mother's,
your mother's as a young woman
walking straight-backed past the Nazi soldiers
to the store to buy cheese and bread for the Jews
she was hiding in the basement,
which is why, I was led to understand,
your father fell in love with her.

The Arrival

In a way, her son, eight,
is my father.

She is not new here.
A number of times she has made my apartment Menschlich
with her mop, broom, and rags.
By necessity, Mr. Clean was one of her first acquaintances.

The things I own are still many years out of her reach,
but she shows no jealousy.
Nothing in her manner demonstrates any Biblical coveting.
Quietly she scrubs the tub,
and she is not offended when I overpay.
All this is temporary to her;
she works with purpose and vision
and looks to the future with hope.

The chances are, I will be very old
by the time she will own a rug as expensive as mine.

Because our languages barely meet
(my Spanish from *El Camino Real*, her English from traffic signs,
storefront sales posters, television, and other immigrant minimums),
I find it hard to explain
which sponges she should use for which dishes,
which is why I buy new ones each time before she comes,
to be faithful to my own.
For once, speech, by its absence, serves its purpose:
with other homes to clean this afternoon,
she has no time to spare,
and I have no energy to articulate the real questions, like
Did your priest tell you we killed Christ?
no way to explain how,
with luck and a great-uncle already a shop owner,
how my ancestors were sponsored just in time
and how her death squads were my Grandpa's Cossacks.
She has no need of my stories. Not now.
I pass on asking her
the Salvadoran equivalent of "greenhorn".

A Hearing Heart

This week I saw her again,
in between our scheduled cleanings.
It was the day her son arrived,
after the puzzling papers were filed and filed again,
after the year and a half of penny pinching,
after the borrowing for the tickets
and fees for the forms and registrations,
after the new torture of waiting
for finicky, flippant approval in the capitals.

Whatever she has made of me,
in a way, her son, eight,
is my father.

A Short Modern History of European Jews

Money for two, yes.
No money for four.
Zeyde had a modest store
and sent them for two,
his cousins,
but they needed more:
about to be married,
they needed four,
which Zeyde didn't have.
The money came back.
They stayed.
(This was 1919.
How bad could it have been?)
They died
(it was 1939)
too fast to leave letters,
for the price of two tickets
my Zeyde didn't have.

The Ukrainian Church

Though she missed her chance,
I understand if her mind was elsewhere.
Her reading pleasantly received by the students the night before,
her heart may well have been light that day,
Still, of all people
— her own mother's mother legs broken in a pogrom —
she should have recognized the scene.
Instead, she turned away.
For her, the church she saw
as her host drove her around that quaint college town
was no more to her than a fragment of lines about Spring,
"...the trees all bright in their white blossoms,
the church beyond,
domed golden,
the bakery nearby,
an aromatic surge of pastries fresh from the ovens."
No more than that.

But I know the church, know it well.
I used to pass it twice a week on the way to class,
some of its worshippers descendants of the men
who crippled her grandmother on a drunken spree
one Lenten season in the Old Country years back.
One of them served her her sweet roll in that shop
which her new poem describes as rich and delicious.
When she washed it down with strong coffee,
she made a note,
"...so fresh, yet gentle, like new love".

Now this poet must set things right:
Go back to the church.
It is more than background for the trees in bloom
that you should have seen;
you, of all, should have seen the bodies in the snow,
and the smell of cakes and doughnuts
should have stunk to the highest Heavens in your nostrils
in that charming little college town
where you were once so cordially invited
to recite your poetry.

Those Who Have The Right

Those who have the right to use "Auschwitz" in a sentence
may use it:
survivors and their families;
some historians who probe the documents in good faith
and know these are the records of human lives and deaths,
that, behind the words, they are Jews who have died;
and their students, in questions for clarification;
one or two poets, but only after great hesitation and forethought,
and only if they use it no more than
three or four times in their careers;
prosecuting attorneys quoting the misuse of the term,
the word, the place, the obscenity,
at the trial of the likes of skinheads
and revisionists and white-collar antisemites
trying to make it acceptable again to do it to the Jews;
Nazi hunters;
some thinkers who have an abundance of mental resilience
and emotional reserve
and who believe in the future of the Jewish people.

Few others.

Nearing the Twentieth Anniversary
of My First and Only Trip to Poland:
Considering Why I Didn't Visit
My Ancestors' Village

There would have been no Jews any more, of course,
had been none for years.
At most, I might have seen shadow outlines of Mezuzahs
on a few doors in one part of the town,
and only if the owners were away
would I have dared approach a house.
Who knows what would have happened
if I had begun running my fingers over the doorposts
and someone had peeked through the curtains?
I would have been fifty miles from Warsaw and the Embassy,
a very long fifty miles,
and it felt like I was in a different century.
The police would have been more on their own out there,
would have been able to do with me as they pleased.

There would have still been tombstones to be seen, yes.
Some of them were in the cemetery perhaps,
the others, face up or down in pieces in the sidewalks
and some of the roads.
A witness in the Fifties had seen them and told others.

There *is* that one chance I would have seen the name "Siegel"...

if rain and snow and wind
hadn't eaten away even their names by then,
or the folk hadn't smashed them so small in their rage and joy
and scattered them
that it would have taken weeks
to find a tantalizing few letters in one place,
the rest, with too much luck to expect, perhaps blocks away,
if still legible at all — names dismembered —
like when people cut up old, invalid credit cards
into smaller and smaller pieces
because they wouldn't want a thief to lay his hands
on the names or numbers for disreputable purposes.

The map shows it would have taken less time
to drive from my hotel to Chorzele,
home of my ancestors, my home,
than from my apartment in Washington to Baltimore,
where I often go just for an night out with friends
without thinking twice about the distance.
Even if the weather turned wicked,
how long could it have taken? At most, an hour.
An hour or two there, and back to Warsaw
with more than enough time left for what needed to be seen
of the ghetto memorial and cemetery.

But I was alone,
and, even twenty years ago,
for anyone to have remembered my Zeyde
he or she would have had to have been over eighty,
if any of them wanted to remember him at all,
and I didn't speak Polish
and my German —
which they would not have wanted to hear in the first place —
had too much Yiddish in it
and it would have given me away
and they would have passed the word around
and kept away from me,
and, besides, why would they want to remember
a mighty young man, handsome in those days perhaps,
who did little more than haul huge crates of cargo
and load them on huge carts all day
to make a living, marry, have three daughters,
pray twice in the daytime and once at night
in a synagogue long torn down
or turned into some public building for the Communist bureaucracy?
My Zeyde,
weary of body from the work
and of soul from the despair —
why would they have remembered my Zeyde?

And besides, I was alone in Poland,
and, at that, never one for great personal courage,
which is why I finally passed on the family excursion
until I could return with someone else, for safety's sake,
something I have not yet done these twenty years,
but will, now that travel is freer,
even if the citizens are not any more hospitable to Jews
than they had been in the past.
I will have to do that sometime, return,
before the Winters gorge on the fading names of my relatives
who have a responsibility for my welfare,
if the Winters ever get milder over there
and not stay the monsters they had always been for centuries
for the Jews.

For that first trip, though,
I had to content myself with the cemetery,
and with some extra time,
a few minutes where the ghetto once stood,
and, of course, my day in Auschwitz.

On a Jewish Tour of Spain

I had come along, Ashkenazi as I am,
only because a friend had said it would be eye-opening,
and besides, as a teacher, I owed it to my students.
It would give me a better understanding of Jewish history.
He scolded me for dwelling too much on Kristallnacht and Nuremberg.

By the third day, it began to feel like
the underground Russia of the Seventies.
The waitress in one of the restaurants asked if one of us was a rabbi,
and even though we told her No, she still asked
why her mother always laid a white cloth on the table Friday nights,
and never touched money until sunset the next day
while everyone else was out shopping.

I was reading some Israeli poet at the time
and, on my strolls, often carried it in my hand.
Many times strangers stopped me, excused themselves,
then asked if the letters were Hebrew and what did it sound like,
moving on in their excitement
to the Israeli team coming to the Olympics in the summer
or crazier subjects like:
Wasn't it strange that one's grandparents, pure Spaniards,
never spoke the names Ferdinand and Isabella
and why so many women in the family
were called by the Castillian form of Ruth and Sara.

In Toledo, our guide asked to borrow the star
I was wearing on a chain around my neck.
She wanted to show it to her children
and promised to return it the next day.
Besides, she added, her father would also like to see it.

In the synagogue, we heard many people fumbling with the melodies,
as if they were trying to remember something,
or *should be* trying to remember.
They were easy to pick out of the congregation:
their eyes were wandering everywhere in wonderment.
It was a look far beyond idle curiosity.

Afterwards, out in the warm noonday sun,
it seemed half of Spain was Jewish,
which at the time seemed in a way so unfair,
Poland being so *judenrein* and cold,
and still blaming its Jews,
dead, Lo, these fifty years.

Israel

Ulpan, Bet Level

For Mark Stadler,
Graduate of Ulpan, Bet Level,
Pride of Gimel.

"Mother and father went to the movies,
but I stayed home."

"I am going to the movies,
while mother and father stay home."

"Mother will be going to the movies,
Father to the café,
but I am staying home tonight."

Now, again, class, all together:
"Abba V'Eema..."
Decline with all your heart,
conjugate with all your soul,
nurse the words with all your might.

The Soup Was Rich Enough

The soup was rich enough,
though not quite as warm as I like when I make it at home.
I prefer it steaming.

This was a new place, and the service was polite, if slow,
and we might have returned at some other time
to the pleasant tables outside
were it not for the bomb squad down the street,
which put a hex on the entire row of restaurants.

First came the cordon of police,
then soldiers — kids, all of them, kids — telling the strollers
in command-mode voice to take another way around.
(We didn't have to move.
The demarcation was beyond us,
which meant, I suppose,
we were out of range of whatever was suspect.)

It was at that moment the scene became more movie-like,
and we found it difficult to comment on the sauces
and whether or not the fish was suitably moist after grilling.
Others at the next table
(I would suspect they were from the neighborhood)
picked up their conversations where they had left off
and went on with their meals
as if this were a part of the local color
as the specialist in mask and chest protector
moved the package this way and that by sight and feel.
I suppose it was because I am not used to bomb scares
I let my mind wander in defense,
and, out of context as it was, I couldn't help thinking that —
if everyone looked in the faces of his or her neighbor
with as much intensity, touched with such care —
we would all be the better for it.

The man in the mask — a boy, really —
had his steps all in order, all timed,
each move and moment with their contingencies
should all hell begin to scatter in the air.
My friend said,
"These are people who are only alive
when they are in touch with danger.
They love to hug death,
and whether or not they have rehearsed the scene
with the ambulance lights flashing
and the search for hands no longer there
is a very individual thing.
Some do and some don't."

I thought of the young boy's mother and father,
and maybe a sister or sweetheart,
and what they must pray for
and to what kind of God
every night when their son or brother or boyfriend
leaves for work downtown.

So it was the three of us:
myself with the soup,
the one with the salad and its pungent mustard dressing
who explained about boys who hug death
whenever the need is felt,
and the third, who had only joined us for dessert
and which he never ate.
We recognized the all clear when, five meters away,
customers at the other restaurants returned to their pasta,
now cold and gone mushy,
and a small number of the strollers continued their walk
by the same route they had planned the night before,
down the very same street,
while most turned back and took an alternate through the alley,
away from the Evil Eye
wrapped in a package
no larger than some slender book of love poems
like Browning's *Sonnets from the Portuguese*
intended for a friend
in Tel Aviv.

And If There Were a Thing Such As Chance

And if there were a thing such as chance,
I might be farming a hundred acres in Wisconsin
or the bearer of gruesome news —
a plastic bomb in an envelope from Belfast.
If there is chance,
would I be sitting here and writing of Jerusalem?

Who is to say — if things just happen —
I would or wouldn't,
at this moment be describing the Rajah's jewels,
or, minus a leg, extending my Hindu arm,
to beg for a near-worthless rupee,
to wolf down a small, half-rotten bowl of peas and rice,
to be buried brown by fire
or floated down the river, unspeakably filthy?

Were things just so,
would I not be hours by night light
poring over Tibetan Holy Books instead of Torah
and toiling by day over a tiny plot of earth
under the great mountains?

But I say no,
though it is simple enough to warm oneself
by the comfortable, fiery Rule of Randomness.

I say no.
Today I hold no hoe, no hand grenade,
no dreams of Ireland free of the Queen's dominion
dear as life itself to myself,
enough for my life or early martyrdom.
The rubies of the Punjab do not hold my interest
any more than starlings or varieties of grapes.
They are little more to me than
"some new things to know about if I find the time."

And so I am here in *my* Jerusalem,
saddled with Jewish history,
yoked with no one else's despair and sufferings,
and rejoicing in my people's dreams come true.
And for good reasons, whatever they may be,
and whether I will ever come to know them or not,
they are mine.

Not Much To Report

Not much to report.
It is barely worth writing you about, but since you insist:
The window of my bedroom faces the wrong way
to catch the morning sunlight when I awaken;
The angles are all unfortunate,
so I see nothing of the street
or the shoppers in the pharmacy out front,
or the children tossing or kicking a ball,
or the reasons for the argument I heard since nine o'clock
from across the courtyard.
What I have here in my side view is
a simple drainpipe, rusting with age.
Where it connects to the wall,
some sprouting, tenacious weed, offspring of the wind,
has broken through.
Further back, outside the next apartment,
a towel already dry still flaps on the line.
Its colors have been dulled
by many too many hours in the sun.
There is a small yard with vegetation in disarray.
One pine's green needles flourish from ground to top,
its neighbor, dead of the old age unique to trees.
Of all details in the frame, only one is "pretty",
and you insist on pretty things:
A trellis around the neighbor's balcony,
lines and leaves, vines and clinging green
grown thick over years,
and here and there in the plant's surprising patterns,
morning glories spray their purples with Impressionistic dots.
(Seurat would have spent many afternoons here.)
Just beyond, a man at his table between color and color
sits in his undershirt and shorts,
sipping tea and stroking a long-haired cat.
It is barely worth writing about.
Just some European refugee, perhaps mid-fifties and free at last,
having his tea at leisure.

Prayer for Intimacy

The way one reads a line that describes Queen Anne's lace
then, reading done, with a casual pointing on a stroll,
a companion says, "There, see, Queen Anne's lace in bloom,
down to the left below the tree line, at the water's edge",
but the fence intrudes, and you promised yourself
you would get your glasses changed months ago but never did,
so, from the distance, the colors wash and lines blur;
or after years of art classes how one examined the classics
from prints and reproductions
and now one stands outside the Louvre
where the oils hang in the flesh,
but it is after hours
because the plane was late coming in
and the next one out leaves before the museum re-opens —
May this trip to Israel, O Guardian and Guide,
be without blur and mishap.
Let me no longer stand one step away from Israel.
Let what my eyes see be real,
without strain or frustration.
Let the Land and People be real and true like when,
in the auditorium after the first rescue of Ethiopians
no seats were left,
and the thin black man had to squeeze so close to me
we were elbow-to-elbow touching,
brothers.

A Dream: A Touch of Glory

Last night,
what I dreamed was
I was just off my rotation in pediatrics at Hadassah,
and I was exhausted.
Then someone pulled me abruptly out of bed,
and, in a police car, I was rushed to the airport
to one of those mammoth planes taking off every few minutes
for Addis Ababa.
I remember being too tired
to be sick from the terrible air pockets
on the flight all the way down.

Then, all of a sudden, we were on the ground,
and, with the same suddenness,
the plane filled to what I thought was overload,
though it was all done in orderly fashion.
They were sitting on the floor,
packed tightly from one wall of the huge cargo bay to the other.
It was difficult to move among them
to attempt even the most elementary examinations.
While others attended to the births,
I looked at the eyes of the old men and women,
checked for infections and wounds on the nearest limbs
I was able to reach,
and bandaged whatever couldn't wait until we landed.
With two hours still to go,
I found an infant, perhaps six weeks old
(though it was hard to tell for certain
because of how they had been living the last few months).
She had one baby foot over the Line of Death.
I did what I could with the few instruments and ointments
I managed to grab in the rush from my dorm,
and prayed for her,
before moving on to the next one
in this sublime and terrifying scene of family triage.

Then, all of a sudden
(this was a dream)
it was the year 2014,
and the place was some college graduation,
and there she stood,
diploma tucked away safely in her skirt pocket,
scanning the crowd for my miraculous hands.

Operation Solomon

The aftermath is not the point today.
Today it is the saving.

You sound like someone who,
still in the middle of a first kiss,
sees bills piling up, tuition,
the family car dead on its tires of old age,
a vacation ruined by a typhoon.

Do not rob us of this moment's wonder by reminding us:
Housing — where will they live?
Who will pay for their teachers and doctors?
Where will all the jobs come from?
Who will cover the costs of all that jet fuel?

From Moment One there were problems,
most certainly will be more,
but the point you insist on missing is:
they are safe and free.
A half-dozen babies were born on the flight,
their first glimpse of life a blurred belly of a cargo plane.

Who will clothe them? you ask.
Ask tomorrow.
Tonight we celebrate.

Glossary

(H=Hebrew; Y=Yiddish)

Abba (H): father.

Alef (H): the first letter of the Hebrew alphabet. Alef-Bet=the alphabet.

Aliya (H): literally "going up". "Making Aliya" = moving to Israel. (Israel was considered higher than all other countries.)

Ashkenazi (H): a descendant of European Jews (except Spain and Portugal, who are Sefardim.)

Baal Shem Tov (H): founder of the Chassidic movement.

Ben (H): son of.

Bet (H): second letter of the Hebrew alphabet and 1st letter of the Torah.

Bobbe (Y): grandmother.

Bracha (H): a blessing.

Challah (H): twisted loaves of bread eaten on the Sabbath and holidays.

Chassidic (H): referring to a Jewish religious movement founded in Eastern Europe in the 18th century by the Baal Shem Tov. Chassidism is known for its sense of joy and ecstasy, particularly manifested in prayer, song, and dance. Chassid: a member of a Chassidic group.

Eema (H): mother.

Essrog: a citrus gruit, used as a ritual object along with a Lulav for various ceremonies on the holiday of Sukkot.

Forverts (Y): a Yiddish newspaper.

Hadassah (H): Medical school in Jerusalem.

Haggadah (H): Hebrew text of the Passover Seder.

Havdalah (H): ceremony on Saturday night (at the end of the Sabbath), separating the Sabbath from the rest of the week. A candle, wine, and spices are used in the ceremony.

Judenrein (German): "clean of Jews". A Nazi term meaning all Jews have been killed in a specific geographic area

Kaddish (H): prayer in memory of the dead, praising God, but not mentioning death.

Kind (Y): a child.

Kiddush (H): the blessing over wine; also the food served in synagogue after Sabbath services.

Kol Nidre (Aramaic): a prayer recited the evening of Yom Kippur as the Holy Day begins.

Kristallnacht (German): November 9-10, 1938, the night the Nazis burned synagogues throughout Germany. ("The Night of Broken Glass.)

Latkes (Y): potato pancakes; Channukah food.

Lulav (h): ritual object composed a palm branch, willows, and myrtle, used in the synagogue and home for the holiday of Sukkot.

Matzah (H): unleavened bread eaten on Passover.

Maidanek: Nazi deathcamp in Poland.

Mauthausen: Nazi deathcamp in Austria.

Mensch (Y; pl.- Menschen, adj.-Menschlich; abs.-Menschlichkeit): an upright, responsible, decent, caring, compassionate person.

Mezuzot (H-pl.; sing.-Mezuzah): a small container holding an inscription from the Torah that is hung on the doorposts of Jewish houses, according to instructions in Deuteronomy Chapter 6.

Mitzvah (H): literally "commandment" or "instruction" — good deeds done by people according to the prescriptions of traditional Jewish texts, such as visiting the sick, comforting mourners, and giving Tzedakah. In this book, Mitzvah is usually synonymous with Tzedakah. (See chapter called "Terminology" at beginning of book.)

Motzi (H): the blessing over bread.

Operation Solomon: 36-hour rescue of Ethiopian Jews, Spring, 1991.

Peretz, Y.L. ((H-Y): famous Yiddish writer.

Pesach (H): Passover

Purim (H): Jewish holiday celebrating the victory of the Jews of Persia over the wicked Haman. The holiday is celebrated with great joy, dancing, parades, masks, and merrymaking.

Pushka (Y): a Tzedakah box.

Rashi (H): Medieval Biblical and Talmudic commentator.

Rebbi (H-Y): teacher *par excellence*, not necessarily a rabbi. Also, a leader of a Chassidic sect.

Seder (H): Passover-night ritual reviewing the Exodus from Egypt.

Seraphim (H, pl. Sing.- Seraph): a type of angel.

Sha (Y): be quiet. Also, "Sha Shtill."

Shabbat/Shabbas (H, Y=Shabbas): the Sabbath.

Shehecheyanu (H): a blessing expressing gratitude to have lived to reach a certain joyous occasion.

Shema (H): the central prayer of Jewish worship.

Shiva (H): literally "seven". The 7 days of moruning when the mourners remain in their home. Religious services are held, and comforters come to express their words of consolation.

Shoah (H): the Holocaust.

Shofar (H): ram's horn, sounded on the High Holidays as a call to repentance.

Shtetl (Y): a village.

Shul (Y): synagogue.

Siddur (H): a prayerbook.

Simcha (H): joy, a joyous occasion.

Simcha Shel Mitzvah (H): the joy of doing Mitzvahs.

Sukkah (H): a flimsy boothlike structure where traditional Jews live during the days of the Sukkot Festival.

Sukkot (H): the Fall festival celebrating a good harvest and commemorating God's kindness to the Children of Israel during their wanderings in the wilderness.

Talitot (H-pl.; sing.-Talit); Y-Tallis): a shawl-like garment with ritual fringes (Tzitzit) on the four corners, worn by Jews during morning prayers.

Talmud (H): an immense compendium of discussions, tales, aphorisms, legal give-and-take, and insights about Judaism, developed in Jewish academies (Yeshivas) during the first five centuries of the Common Era.

Torah (H): literally "teaching". Originally meaning the Five Books of Moses, expanded to include the entirety of Jewish study and learning. "To talk Torah" is to discuss these texts.

Tzaddik (H; pl.-Tzaddikim): a righteous person

Tzedakah (H): the distinctly Jewish method of performing charitable acts. From the word "Tzedek", Justice.

Tzitzit (H): ritual fringes on the corners of a Tallit (prayer-shawl).

Ulpan (H): intensive program for learning Hebrew.

Yiddishkeit (Y): Judaism.

Yom Kippur (H): the Day of Atonement.

Zeyde (Y): a grandfather.

DANNY SIEGEL is a free-lance author, poet, and lecturer who resides in Rockville, Maryland, when not on his speaking tours or in Israel distributing Tzedakah monies.

For more than a decade, he has concentrated most of his writings on Tzedakah, attempting to focus the public's attention on the deeds of loving-kindness. *Mitzvahs*, published in 1990, was the latest in this essay series. His previous works on Tzedakah: *Munbaz II and Other Mitzvah Heroes, Gym Shoes and Irises, Books One and Two*, have become the standard guideline text for personalized tzedakah.

His publication of *Family Reunion: Making Peace in the Jewish Community*, addressed the painful subject of disunity and polarization, making an attempt to sows the seeds of harmony.

The Meadow Beyond The Meadow, published in 1991, was Danny's sixth book of poetic writings, first begun in 1969 with the publication of *Soulstoned*, a collector's item now out of print. Following on the heels on *Meadow's* remarkable success, Danny has created *A Hearing Heart*.

Siegel is a popular lecturer at synagogues, Jewish federations, community centers, conventions, and retreats, where he teaches Tzedakah and Jewish values and recites from his works. His books and talks have received considerable acclaim throughout the entire North American Jewish community.